Heroes
of the
Revolution

by DAVID A. ADLER

illustrated by
DONALD A. SMITH

HOLIDAY HOUSE / New York

In memory of
my brother Eddie (1948–1979),
a hero for my generation.
He gave his life to save another.
D. A. A.

To Kirk and Angie
D. A. S.

The heroes profiled here were selected only as examples
of the many brave and diverse heroes of the Revolution.

With special thanks to Andrew Batten,
director of the Fraunces Tavern Museum, for his help

Library of Congress Cataloging-in-Publication Data
Adler, David A.
Heroes of the Revolution / by David A. Adler; illustrated by Donald A. Smith.—1st ed.
p. cm.
Includes bibliographical references.
ISBN 0-8234-1471-X
1.United States—History—Revolution, 1775–1783—Biography—Juvenile literature.
2. Revolutionaries—United States—Biography—Juvenile literature.
3. Statesmen—United States—Biography—Juvenile literature.
[1. United States—History—Revolution, 1775–1783—Biography.]
I. Smith, Donald A., ill. II. Title.

E206.A25 2003
973.3'092'2—dc21
[B]
00-038843

ISBN-13: 978-0-8234-1471-0 (hardcover)   ISBN-10: 0-8234-1471-X (hardcover)
ISBN-13: 978-0-8234-2017-9 (paperback)   ISBN-10: 0-8234-2017-5 (paperback)

Contents

Ethan Allen
(1738–1789)

———◆◆———

Ethan Allen of Vermont was a big man. At six feet, six inches tall, he was almost a full foot taller than the average British soldier. The British called him the American Giant.

On May 10, 1775, in the first American attack of the Revolutionary War, Ethan Allen and Benedict Arnold led a troop of soldiers, the Green Mountain Boys, over a wall of Fort Ticonderoga in New York.

The first British guard to spot the invading Patriots shot his musket, but the gun misfired. A second guard pointed a bayonet at Allen and his troops. Allen hit the guard on his head and called to the British commander, "Come out, you old rat!" An officer appeared with his uniform coat on, but without his pants. "Surrender the fort!" Allen demanded of him. "In the name of the Great Jehovah and the Continental Congress."

Allen took Fort Ticonderoga without firing a shot. He and his troops captured large cannons, cannonballs, and other ammunition, which were later used to force the British out of Boston.

Crispus Attucks
(1723?–1770)

———————•◆•———————

Crispus Attucks, "'the first to defy', . . . the first to die" in the American Revolution, had been a slave in Framingham, Massachusetts. He escaped in 1750, but little else is known about his life before March 5, 1770. That night he was in Boston, on King Street. He was one of a large group of Americans who crowded around a troop of British soldiers, calling them "lobsters" and "bloody backs" because of their red uniforms. The Patriots threw snow and chunks of ice at the soldiers. Crispus Attucks stepped forward, holding a thick piece of wood. "Attack the main guard! Strike at the root!" Attucks called to the others. "Shoot if you dare!" he yelled at the soldiers.

The soldiers shot.

The *Boston Gazette* reported that Attucks was hit with two bullets and "killed instantly . . . most horribly." That night, in what was later called the Boston Massacre, Attucks and four others were the first to die in the struggle for American independence.

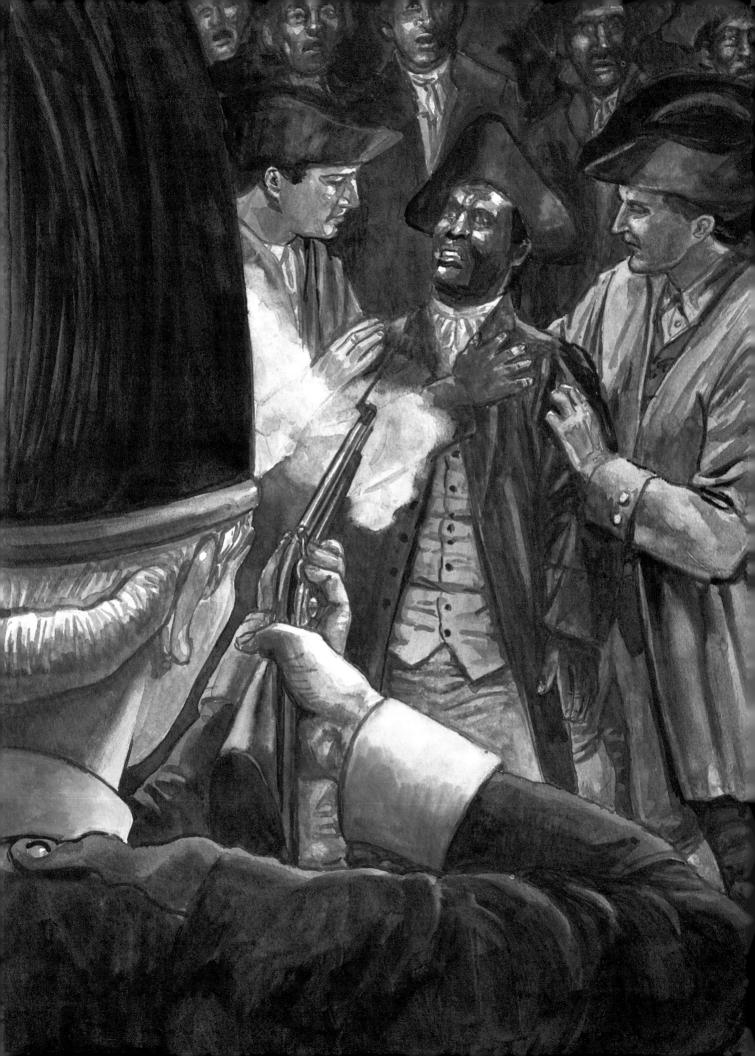

Lydia Darragh
(1729–1789)

———◆———

Lydia Darragh was born in Ireland. In 1753 she came to the American colonies with her husband, William.

Lydia Darragh was a small woman, just five feet tall. Her neighbors knew her as a mother of five and a nurse. Few people knew she was also a spy for the Continental army.

In 1777 the British occupied Philadelphia. General Howe, the commander of the British army, made his headquarters on Second Street, in the house next door to the Darraghs'. Howe and his officers used the Darragh house for meetings, and Lydia Darragh hid in a linen closet and spied on them.

On December 2, 1777, Lydia Darragh heard the British plan a surprise attack on the Continental army. The next morning she left Second Street, carrying an empty flour bag. She told British guards she was going to fill it with flour at a nearby mill. Instead, she hurried toward the Patriot troops, some thirteen miles away. She told one of Washington's soldiers of Howe's plans, and the British attack failed.

The British knew they had been betrayed. A few days later they questioned Lydia Darragh. They soon released her. They could not believe this small woman had caused their defeat.

Nathan Hale
(1755–1776)

———•———

Soon after the battles of Lexington and Concord, Nathan Hale, a Connecticut teacher, joined the American cause. By 1776 he was an officer, and in September he volunteered to spy on the British. He told a friend, "I wish to be useful."

Hale disguised himself as a Dutch schoolmaster and moved among the enemy. He drew pictures of their camp, took notes, and hid the notes in his shoes. On his way back to General Washington, he was caught. The next day, without a trial, Nathan Hale was hanged.

A ladder was set against an apple tree. A noose was tied from a sturdy branch, and British soldiers gathered to see the American spy hang. According to an 1800s report, "With the rope around his neck, and Eternity before him, the young man was very pale, but calm, collected and firm." Before dying, he called to the hangman to "witness that he had but one regret. . . . said the martyr, 'I only regret that I have but one life to lose for my country.'"

Mary "Molly Pitcher" Hays
(1754–1832)

In 1775, when the fight for independence began, a barber named John Caspar Hays joined the Continental army. His wife, Mary, went along to cook, wash, and sew for the troops.

On June 28, 1778, John and Mary Hays were in New Jersey at the battle of Monmouth. It was one of the longest battles of the war, on perhaps the hottest day of the year. Mary saw the men suffering from the heat and grabbed a pitcher. She filled it with water and ran among the men, giving them drinks.

"Molly!" the men called to get her attention. "Molly! Pitcher!"

Mary's husband fell from the heat. She gave him a drink, tied a wet rag around his head, and moved him beneath a tree. Then she took over her husband's place, stood there in her dress, and helped the crew load and fire the cannon.

A witness later wrote about Mary, "While in the action of reaching a cartridge and having one of her feet as far before the other as she could step, a cannon shot from the enemy passed directly between her legs without doing any other damage than carrying away the lower part of her petticoat."

When others ran from battle, Mary Hays stood fast. She was still there, holding off the British, when General Washington checked the retreat.

Thomas Jefferson
(1743–1826)

———•———

Thomas Jefferson was a farmer, lawyer, architect, musician, and inventor. Before the Revolution he was a member of Virginia's House of Burgesses; later, he would become president of the United States. He was a writer, too. His pen was a powerful tool in America's fight for independence.

In 1776 Jefferson wrote the Declaration of Independence. It marked the colonies' formal break with England and was approved and adopted by the Second Continental Congress on July 4, 1776.

Jefferson wrote in the Declaration, "We hold these truths to be self-evident, that all men are created equal, that they are endowed by their Creator with certain unalienable Rights, that among these are Life, Liberty, and the pursuit of Happiness."

He wrote that King George III had "plundered our seas, ravaged our Coasts, burnt our towns, and destroyed the lives of our people," and that governments are meant to serve people, not be served by them. Jefferson called the king a tyrant, "unfit to be the ruler of a free people," and because all appeals to the king had failed, Jefferson declared that only one course of action remained: independence.

John Paul Jones
(1747–1792)

———•———

John Paul Jones, the great American naval officer, was born in Scotland. There, he was a ship's captain. In 1773, after he killed one of his men during a mutiny, he fled to America. Two years later, when the Revolutionary War broke out, Jones joined the new American navy in the fight against the British.

On September 23, 1779, Jones's ship, the *Bon Homme Richard*, sailed within one hundred yards of the *Serapis*, an enemy warship. Jones raised an American flag.

Sailors on the *Serapis* fired their guns.

"The battle being thus begun," Jones wrote later, "was continued with unremitting fury."

The quicker British ship sailed around the *Bon Homme Richard* and first fired at her stern, then at her starboard side. Fifty-nine of the American ship's sixty-two guns were disabled. The vessel was on fire and sinking.

The Americans' plight seemed desperate, but Jones did not surrender. According to one legend, he called to the enemy, "I have not yet begun to fight!"

An American sailor threw a grenade onto the *Serapis* and set off some ammunition. The explosion destroyed the enemy ship's main deck, and it was the British who surrendered to John Paul Jones.

Thomas Paine
(1737–1809)

Thomas Paine was born in England, where he was a teacher, corset maker, grocer, and tobacco dealer. He came to America just before the outbreak of the Revolutionary War and was soon caught up in the anti-British fervor. He said later, "The cause of America made me an author."

Paine wrote the pamphlet *Common Sense*, which was published in 1776. It sold more than one hundred thousand copies. In it Paine declared, "A government of our own is our natural right." He wrote that it was better to live in America where the "law is king" than in Britain where "the king is law."

"Tyranny . . . is not easily conquered," Paine warned, "yet we have this consolation . . . the harder the defeat, the more glorious the triumph."

George Washington was so stirred by Paine's arguments that he read aloud from *Common Sense* to inspire his troops.

Paine's words fired the spirits of American Patriots during these times—"times," Paine wrote, "that try men's souls."

Paul Revere
(1735–1818)

———•———

Paul Revere was a silversmith, an engraver, and a maker of eyeglasses and false teeth. He was also a staunch Patriot set on rebellion. He created political cartoons to incite Americans to rebel, and he took part in the Boston Tea Party in 1773.

Two years later Revere learned that British soldiers were about to attack Patriots at Lexington and Concord, Massachusetts. Late at night, on April 18, 1775, he got on his horse, outraced two British soldiers, and reached Lexington in time to warn Samuel Adams, John Hancock, and others. When Revere was detained by British scouts, Samuel Prescott went on to warn the people of Concord.

"Through the night rode Paul Revere," the poet Henry Wadsworth Longfellow wrote some time later, "and so through the night went his cry of alarm . . . In the hour of darkness and peril and need, / The people will waken and listen to hear / The hurrying hoof-beats of that steed, / And the midnight message of Paul Revere."

Thanks to Revere and Prescott, the Patriots were ready to defend themselves in the first battles of the Revolution.

Haym Salomon
(1740–1785)

Haym Salomon was born in Poland and fought for its independence. After that effort failed, he fled to America and soon joined the fight for American independence.

Haym Salomon helped hide Patriots. Late one night in 1778, he was moving an injured soldier from his house in British-held New York City to safety behind Patriot lines. He was spotted. Salomon jumped off the wagon and stood in the road so the soldier could escape. For defying British rule, Salomon was arrested and sentenced to die; but the night before his hanging, he escaped.

That was not the end of Salomon's work for independence.

By fall of 1779, Patriot troops, unpaid for months, refused to fight. A plea for help from Robert Morris, financier of the war, reached Salomon, a devout Jew, on Yom Kippur, the solemn day of fasting and prayer. Then and there, in the synagogue, Salomon got pledges for support. That night when the holy day ended, he sent Morris the money he needed. Almost two hundred years later, a citation accompanying a stamp issued in his honor declared that Salomon's work as a financier helped "save the new nation from collapse."

Deborah Sampson
(1760–1827)

Deborah Sampson of Massachusetts was a servant, a farmer, and a Patriot. When General Washington called for men to volunteer for the Continental army, she felt the need to serve.

Sampson dressed as a man and walked more than fifty miles to Worcester, Massachusetts, where she could enlist without having a physical examination. She gave her name as Robert Shurtleff and in May 1782 was made a soldier in the 4th Massachusetts Regiment.

In one battle Sampson was shot in the leg. Though she was in pain, she continued to fight. When she was alone, using just a penknife and needle, she removed the bullet. But in October 1783, Deborah Sampson fell ill. She became unconscious with a high fever. A doctor examined her and discovered she was a woman. Deborah Sampson was soon discharged from the army with honor.

When she died in 1827, both her name and the name she took, Robert Shurtleff, were put on her tombstone followed by the epitaph "The female soldier."

George Washington
(1732–1799)

By 1775 George Washington of Virginia had been a surveyor, farmer, and statesman. He had been a soldier, too. In the 1750s he was an officer in the Virginia militia. He fought for the British in the French and Indian Wars. On June 15, 1775, George Washington was unanimously elected commander of the Continental army by the delegates to the Second Continental Congress. He accepted, he said, to support "the glorious cause."

The Continental army was made up of mostly untrained, poorly armed men. They were expected to battle the army of the most powerful country in the world.

Washington ordered no "profane cursing, swearing or drunkenness" among his men and insisted that they attend religious services and "implore the blessings of heaven." He reminded his officers that when they "set good examples, it may be expected that the men will with zeal and alacrity follow them."

Washington held the army together. He lead it to triumph over the British at Yorktown, Virginia. When the British prime minister learned of his nation's defeat there, he cried out, "Oh, God, it's all over!"

And it was.

Yorktown was the last great battle of the Revolutionary War. General George Washington had led the Continental army to victory.

Author's Notes

Ethan Allen was born in Connecticut. He later settled in a section of New Hampshire that is now Vermont.

Israel Harris, who was at the battle of Fort Ticonderoga, claimed Ethan Allen shouted unrepeatable curse words, not that he took the fort in "the name of the Great Jehovah and the Continental Congress."

Benedict Arnold, who led the attack on Fort Ticonderoga with Ethan Allen, turned traitor in 1780 and joined the British forces.

It is likely that Crispus Attucks, recognized as the first African-American hero of the Revolution, was at least part American Indian.

Following the Boston Massacre, the British captain and his troops were tried for murder, with John Adams and Josiah Quincy as their lawyers. Just two soldiers were convicted. Their right thumbs were burned with a branding iron and the men were released.

It was so hot at the battle of Monmouth that at least one hundred soldiers, American and British, died from the heat.

The British tried to capture signers of the Declaration of Independence. Nine signers were killed in fighting. Five were captured by the British. The homes of twelve others were destroyed. But none of the fifty-six signers renounced his support for the Declaration.

John Paul Jones's ship was named the *Bon Homme Richard* (French for "Poor Richard") to honor Benjamin Franklin, who wrote *Poor Richard's Almanack*.

According to reports from sailors on the *Bon Homme Richard*, Jones's response to the call to surrender was, "No, I'll sink, but I'll be damned if I'll strike [surrender]." The first written record that his response was "I have not yet begun to fight" was in an 1825 report, written more than forty years after the battle.

In 1836 an act of Congress granted pensions to widows of Continental army soldiers. Benjamin Gannett was granted such a pension for his wife's service.

He was the widower of Deborah Sampson.

At times his role as commander of the Continental army led Washington to despair. In January 1776 he wrote, "I have often thought how much happier I should have been, if, instead of accepting a command under such circumstances, I had taken my musket upon my shoulders and entered the ranks."

Important Dates

October 25, 1760	George II dies. George III becomes king of England.
April 5, 1764	Sugar Act passes, the first tax in the colonies enacted solely to raise money for England.
March 22, 1765	Stamp Act, which taxes printed matter, passes in Parliament.
June 29, 1767	Townshend Acts, taxes on lead, paint, paper, and tea, passed by Parliament.
March 5, 1770	Five Patriots die in the Boston Massacre.
December 16, 1773	Patriots dump 342 chests of tea into Boston Harbor in the Boston Tea Party.
March–June 1774	British Parliament passes the Intolerable Acts.
September 5–October 26, 1774	The First Continental Congress meets in Philadelphia to find a way to settle the colonists' disputes with Britain.
April 19, 1775	The first battle of the war is fought at Lexington and Concord, Massachusetts.
May 10, 1775	The Green Mountain Boys, led by Ethan Allen and Benedict Arnold, capture Fort Ticonderoga from the British.
June 15, 1775	George Washington is appointed commander of the Continental army.

June 17, 1775	Patriot soldiers are forced to retreat at the battle of Bunker Hill in Massachusetts.
January 10, 1776	*Common Sense*, by Thomas Paine, is published.
July 4, 1776	The Declaration of Independence is adopted by the Second Continental Congress.
August 27–28, 1776	The Continental army is defeated in the battle of Long Island, losing New York City to the British.
December 26, 1776 and January 3, 1777	Battles of Trenton and Princeton in New Jersey, two Washington-led Patriot victories, help restore America's hopes.
September 11, 1777	Battle of Brandywine, Pennsylvania, is fought. Patriots lose Philadelphia.
December 19, 1777	Beginning of the difficult winter for Patriot troops at Valley Forge, Pennsylvania.
February 6, 1778	Treaty of Amity and Commerce is signed. France allies with the United States.
June 28, 1778	The British retreat at the battle of Monmouth in New Jersey.
September 23, 1779	Patriot victory in the naval battle of the *Bon Homme Richard* and the British warship *Serapis*.
January 1781	Daniel Morgan leads a Patriot victory in the battle of Cowpens, South Carolina.
October 6–19, 1781	Patriot victory at Yorktown, Virginia.
September 3, 1783	The Treaty of Paris is signed. The British recognize their former colonies as an independent nation.

Source Notes

Each source note includes the first word or words and the last word of a quotation and its source. References are to books cited in the Selected Bibliography.

p. 5 "Come . . . rat!", "Surrender . . . fort!", "In the . . . Congress.": Reeder, p. 6

p. 6 "'the first . . . die": Wilson, p. 31; "Attack . . . root!", "Shoot . . . dare!": Hughes, p. 26; "killed . . . horribly.": Emery, p. 10

p. 10 "I . . . useful.": Boatner, p. 475; "With . . . country.": Lippard, p. 269

p. 13 "While . . . petticoat.": Page Smith, p. 1098

p. 14 "We hold . . . people": *Annals*, pp. 447–449

p. 17 "The battle . . . fury.": Morison, p. 229; "I have . . . fight!": Sobol, p. 103

p. 18 "The cause . . . author.", "A government . . . right.", "law . . . law.", "Tyranny . . . triumph.", "times . . . souls.": *Annals*, pp. 397, 456

p. 21 "Through . . . Revere.": Sobol, pp. 9–12

p. 22 "save . . . collapse.": Milgrim, p. 119

p. 25 "The . . . soldier.": Jesse Carney Smith, p. 975

p. 26 "the . . . cause.", "profane . . . heaven.", "set . . . them.", "Oh . . . over!": Headley, pp. 127–128

Selected Bibliography

Annals of America: Volume Two—Resistance and Revolution. London: Encyclopedia Britannica, 1968.

Banco, Richard L. *The American Revolution, 1775–1783: An Encyclopedia.* New York: Garland, 1993.

Birmingham, Stephen. *The Grandees.* New York: Harper and Row, 1971.

Boatner, Mark Mayo, III. *Encyclopedia of the American Revolution.* New York: David McKay, 1966.

Clyne, Patricia Edwards. *Patriots in Petticoats.* New York: Dodd Mead, 1976.

Davis, Burke. *Black Heroes of the American Revolution.* New York: Harcourt Brace Jovanovich, 1976.

Emery, Edwin. *The Story of America as Reported by its Newspapers.* New York: Simon & Schuster, 1965.

Freeman, Douglas Southall. *George Washington: Leader of the Revolution.* New York: Charles Scribner's Sons, 1951.

Headley, J. T. *The Illustrated Life of George Washington*. New York: G & F Bill, 1860.

Historical Statistics of the United States, Colonial Times to 1970. Washington, D.C.: United States Department of Commerce, 1975.

Holbrook, Stewart H. *Ethan Allen*. New York: Macmillan, 1946.

Hughes, Langston. *Famous Negro Heroes of America*. New York: Dodd Mead, 1958.

Landman, Isaac, ed. *The Universal Jewish Encyclopedia*. New York: Universal Jewish Encyclopedia, Inc., 1943.

Leckie, Robert. *George Washington's War*. New York: HarperCollins, 1992.

Lippard, George. *Washington and His Generals: or Legends of the Revolution*. Philadelphia: G. B. Zieber, 1847.

Milgrim, Shirley. *Haym Salomon: Liberty's Son*. Philadelphia: Jewish Publication Society, 1975.

Moore, Frank. *The Diary of the American Revolution*. New York: Washington Square Press, 1967.

Morison, Samuel Eliot. *John Paul Jones: A Sailor's Biography*. Boston: Little Brown, 1959.

Purvis, Thomas L. *Almanacs of American Life: Revolutionary America, 1763–1800*. New York: Facts on File, 1995.

Quarles, Benjamin. *The Negro in the American Revolution*. Chapel Hill: University of North Carolina Press, 1961.

Reeder, Colonel Red. *Bold Leaders of the American Revolution*. Boston: Little Brown, 1973.

Roberts, Kenneth. *The Battle of Cowpens*. New York: Doubleday, 1958.

Smith, Jesse Carney, ed. *Notable Black American Women*. Detroit: Gale Research, 1992.

Smith, Page. *A New Age Now Begins*. New York: McGraw Hill, 1976.

Sobol, Donald J. *An American Revolutionary War Reader*. New York: Franklin Watts, 1964.

Street, James. *The Revolutionary War*. New York: Dial Press, 1954.

Ward, Christopher. *The War of the Revolution*. New York: Macmillan, 1952.

Wilson, Ruth. *Our Blood and Tears: Black Freedom Fighters*. New York: Putnam, 1972.

Woodward, W. E. *George Washington: The Image and the Man*. New York: Boni and Liveright, 1926.

Zobel, Hiller B. *The Boston Massacre*. New York: W. W. Norton, 1970.